To Loose + Paul

On Your Wedding Day

May these Prayers Be

Comforting & Helpful

In Your New Life

Together.

21 November '08.

POCKET PRAYERS
FOR MARRIAGE

POCKET PRAYERS
FOR MARRIAGE

COMPILED BY
ANDREW AND PIPPA BODY

 CHURCH HOUSE
PUBLISHING

Church House Publishing
Church House
Great Smith Street
London SW1P 3NZ
Tel: 020 7898 1451
Fax: 020 7898 1449

ISBN 0 7151 4018 3

Published 2004 by Church House Publishing

Typeset by Vitaset, Paddock Wood, Kent
Printed in England by the University Printing House,
Cambridge

CONTENTS

PREFACE

These prayers come out of over thirty years of being alongside people in their relationships, and out of our thirty-five years of being husband and wife, Mum and Dad, and now Granny and Granpa.

Prayer can be a very private part of a relationship. Andrew once asked a non-churchgoing couple who were preparing for marriage whether they ever prayed. At that point they had been living together for over five years. The groom-to-be said, 'Yes, I pray every night.' His other half visibly jumped. Andrew said to her, 'You didn't know that, did you?' 'I hadn't the faintest idea.' 'And what about you?' Came the reply: 'I pray every night, too.'

Andrew offered to introduce them to each other. They were so close, and knew each other (they thought) so well. But prayer had been a secret thing for both of them. Whether open or secret, God hears our prayers.

The stories Andrew tells at the beginning of each chapter are not about the famous and the learned, but about the ordinary men and women whom he has had the privilege to know, and who in different ways have experienced something of God in their marriage, and so have

taught us new things worth knowing. Whether
you are about to be married or heading for your
fiftieth anniversary, our prayer is that the ones
included in this book will help and inspire you
in your own. At different times we want to say
'Thank you', 'Sorry' and 'Please' to our partner.
Prayer is one of the ways we say those things
to God.

Andrew and Pippa Body

PREPARING TO BE MARRIED

Most churches offer some form of marriage preparation that goes beyond organizing the wedding, and helps couples to reflect on their decision to marry. For almost all, this will be a time to grow in love and understanding of each other. For just a few, it may be a time to think again, and perhaps to delay marriage until difficulties have been faced and resolved. One bride rang me after our first meeting, during which I had asked them – jokingly – why out of all humanity they had chosen each other. She wanted to call off the wedding. 'I couldn't think of any reason to marry him when you asked us last night – and I still can't think of one today!'

*

What fun it is to plan the wedding day, Lord.
   Walking down the aisle ...
   Standing at the altar ...
   Singing our favourite hymn ...
Aisle ... altar ... hymn ... ?

Andrew Body

This is the biggest decision of my life. If I make the right choice, it could be the best decision of my life. If I make the wrong one, it could be the worst decision of my life. My thoughts are racing so fast I feel exhausted by them. I have feelings that are so powerful, they almost disable me. I am in touch with new and hidden depths within myself. My mind, heart and soul are alive in a way I have never known. Stand with me, and help me to know what to do.

Andrew Body

Lord Jesus Christ, who by your presence and power brought joy to the wedding at Cana: bless those engaged to be married, that there may be truth at the beginning of their lives together, unselfishness all the way, and perseverance to the end. May their hopes be realized and their love for each other deepen and grow, that through them your name may be glorified.

Mothers' Union

That I may come near to her, draw me
nearer to thee than to her; that I may know
her, make me to know thee more than her;
that I may love her with the perfect love of
a perfectly whole heart, cause me to love
thee more than her and most of all.
Amen. Amen.

That nothing may be between me and her,
be thou between us, every moment. That
we may be constantly together, draw us
into separate loneliness with thyself. And
when we meet breast to breast, My God, let
it be on thine own. Amen. Amen.

Temple Gairdner (1873–1928)

Lord of love,
we pray for *N* and *N*.
Be with them in all their preparations
and on their wedding day.
Give them your love in their hearts
throughout their married life together,
through Jesus Christ our Lord.

Common Worship: Pastoral Services

Loving God
we rejoice with A and C
that they are engaged to be married.
Bless these promises they have made:
bless these rings they have given;
and bless this time of preparation they offer
     to each other.
May they come to experience
     a life-long unity of heart, body and mind;
     comfort and companionship;
     enrichment and encouragement;
     tenderness and trust.
We offer our prayer through Jesus Christ
     our Lord.

Vows and Partings

Lord, we are so much in love and spend so
much time thinking about each other. Help
us not to be possessive, but to keep our
wide circle of friends. Help us to grow to
understand each other. Help our love not to
blind us to differences that we must accept

in our own individual uniqueness.
We know that we have to work at our
relationships but we are tempted to think
that everything will just fall into place
and be wonderful. Help us to be open
with each other, and let others share our
great happiness.

Women at Prayer

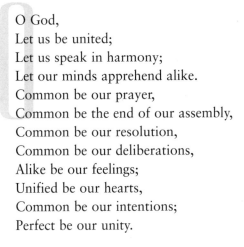

O God,
Let us be united;
Let us speak in harmony;
Let our minds apprehend alike.
Common be our prayer,
Common be the end of our assembly,
Common be our resolution,
Common be our deliberations,
Alike be our feelings;
Unified be our hearts,
Common be our intentions;
Perfect be our unity.

From the Rig-Veda (Hindu Scriptures)

There are so many choices:
   venues and menus
   dresses and tresses
   shades and bridesmaids
   cars and guitars
   houses and blouses
   speeches and preachers.
It is so easy to overspend; to lose all sense
     of proportion.
Help us to plan not only for the day, but
     for the rest of our life.
Help us to choose the best things:
   faith
   hope
   love.

Andrew Body

Lord,
the source of all true love,
we pray for *these couples*.
Grant to them
joy of heart,
seriousness of mind
and reverence of spirit,
that as they enter into the oneness
     of marriage
they may be strengthened and guided
     by you,
through Jesus Christ our Lord.

Common Worship: Pastoral Services

※

THE WEDDING DAY

'When are we actually married?' asked one couple. As a recently ordained priest, it was a question I had never been asked. I have never regretted how I replied. I reminded them that we talk about 'getting married', which implies it is a process, not a magic moment. What the wedding day does is to make a private decision into a very public one that affects everyone. As the Wedding Preface in Common Worship, the Church of England's service book, says: 'Marriage ... enriches society and strengthens community'. So when the bells ring out, they are telling the world that history has been made.

*

At the start of a wedding day

This day has been so long coming,
so long planned,
so long anticipated.
Help us relax enough to enjoy it.
Help us concentrate enough to appreciate it.
Be with those who have a special part to play
and with everyone as they travel to join us.
May this day be all we have hoped for.
May it be a wonderful start to the rest of
    our lives.

Andrew Body

*

God of love,
we thank you for the gift of marriage and
    for the joys it brings.
Bless us as we share in this wedding.
We thank you for the love
which has brought N and N to each other
and for their desire to share that love for
    the rest of their lives;
through Jesus Christ our Lord.

A New Zealand Prayer Book – He Karakia Mihinare O Aotearoa

God of love, ever gracious and kind,
we pray for N and N as they make the
     promises of marriage.
Let them know you
as the God of mercy and new beginnings,
who forgives our failures and renews
     our hope.
May the grace of Christ
be poured into their wedding
for celebration and for joy.
God of love, ever present and faithful,
may N and N know that their marriage is
     your delight and will.
May the promises they make govern their
     life together,
as your presence surrounds them,
and your Spirit strengthens and guides them;
through Jesus Christ our Lord.

Common Worship: Pastoral Services

*

Our marriage starts with a romantic day. Everything is special – clothes unlike any others we ever wear; a unique gathering of friends and families; solemn vows in weighty words. Thank you for all that is special. But help us to know that our marriage is not built on these things, nor on pieces of paper that say what we have done. It is built on what we have been to each other already, and what we want to be for each other in the future. It is built on the sharing of little, everyday things. Those things are special too.

Andrew Body

✳

'For better, for worse; for richer, for poorer;
    in sickness and in health'.
We would be funny people, Lord, if we
    were thinking on our wedding day,
'We are going to be worse and poor
    and sick.'
We want to be saying
'We will be better, richer and healthy.'
So thank you for the reality
    of those promises,
Because we cannot get through life without
    coping with bad things
    as well as good.
We are there for each other,
    whatever may come.
And we know you will be there with us.

Andrew Body

*

O God, whose nature is unending love,
We offer these rings to be blessed.
As we place them upon our fingers,
May we perceive your own hands,
Ready to catch us when we fall,
To caress us when we are tired,
And to lead us laughing to new delights.
So teach us the way of unending love,
That our hearts may be full,
And our lives open to one another,
To your greater glory.

Timothy Woods

＊

We stand, ready to begin the journey.
We cannot see the way ahead;
We do not know what pitfalls there may be.
We believe the companionship we share
Will help us along the way.
We imagine future joys, but only guess
    their greatness.
Come, Spirit of God, come with us.
Be the breath of life we breathe,
The fire of passion that enthrals us,
Come, lead us with hope into the unknown,
To the promise hidden before us.

Timothy Woods

We wouldn't want to change anything about each other, but already we have changed. Our love has helped each of us grow as people. Because we offer each other new strengths and insights, our lives are richer and fuller. Help us to go on giving each other these blessings. We are channels through which your grace comes to each of us. Fill us with that grace every day of our life together.

Andrew Body

Blessings in abundance come,
To the Bride and to her Groom;
May the Bed and this short night,
Know the fullness of delight!
Pleasures many here attend ye,
And, ere long, a Boy love send ye,
Curld and comely, and so trimme,
Maides (in time) may ravish him.
Thus a dew of graces fall
On ye both; Goodnight to all.

Robert Herrick (1591–1674)

Blessed art thou, O Lord our God,
     King of the universe,
who hath created all things to thy glory.
Blessed art thou, O Lord our God,
     King of the universe, Creator of man.
Blessed art thou, O Lord our God,
     King of the universe,
who hast made man in thine image,
          after thy likeness and hast prepared
          unto him, out of his very self,
          a perpetual fabric.
Blessed art thou, O Lord, Creator of man.
O make these loved companions greatly
          to rejoice, even as of old thou didst
          gladden thy creatures in the garden
          of Eden.
Blessed art thou, O Lord, who makest
          bridegroom and bride to rejoice.
Blessed art thou, O Lord our God,
     King of the universe,
who hast created joy and gladness,
          bridegroom and bride, mirth and
          exultation, pleasure and delight, love,
          brotherhood, peace and fellowship.

Soon may there be heard in the cities of
  Judah, and in the streets of Jerusalem,
  the voice of the bridegroom and the
  voice of the bride, the jubilant voice of
  bridegrooms from their canopies, and
  of youths from their feasts of song.
Blessed art thou, O Lord, who makest the
  bridegroom to rejoice with the bride.

The Hebrew Prayer Book

Lord of weddings where the ordinary took on
an extra special flavour
may – and – taste the rich wine of your love.
Let their love be a
listening
forgiving
honest
caring
sharing
a sharing of delight and chores
of good times and bad.
May they go out now with confidence
into the community as a new creation.
Lovers – made in your image.

The Iona Community: from The Pattern of our Days

QUICK PRAYERS AT CHURCH

For the Groom as he waits

Lord, the clock seems to have stopped.
Keep my heart ticking properly.

For the Bride as she enters

Lord, help me not to trip – and keep those
bridesmaids from treading on my dress.

For the Priest, as he begins

This is my twentieth wedding this year, but
their only one. Help me to make it unique
and special.

For the Best Man, as he is asked
for the ring

From holes in the pocket, gratings in
the floor and butter fingers, good Lord
deliver us.

For the Bridesmaid, as she takes
the bouquet

Lord, may these flowers *not* be ones that
make me sneeze.

For the Lesson Reader, as he goes
to the lectern

Lord, I've practised so hard. Please may
I say 'Gentiles' and *not* 'genitals'.

For the Organist, as the end of the
service approaches

Lord, help me to forgive them for asking
for the Widor Toccata.

Andrew Body

*

Eternal God
You are with us
In the fullness of your love:

Love made flesh for us,
Bearing the weight of human guilt and shame;
Love which fills our hearts
And binds us to each other,
Creating communion from separation;
Love which you are willing to renew
    continually
In the lives of N and N.

Make them a sign to us
Of your love in all creation;
Of your forgiveness and self-sacrifice
That gives us hope;
And of our being together, with you
For lasting delight
And indestructible peace.

By your Holy Spirit,
Reveal your glory through us all,
And let the world receive in us
The healing and joy of Christ,
As you keep us in eternal life.

An Order for Marriage for Christians from Different Churches

At the end of a wedding day

Now there are just the two of us.
Thank you for everything we have
    experienced today.
Thank you for all the people who have
    made it what it was.
This is the day we got married;
we will never forget it.
But may we never stop getting married,
never stop giving ourselves to each other,
and growing in love and trust and joy
in all the years ahead.

Andrew Body

*

THE EARLY YEARS

*'I shall never stop getting married', said a
seventeen-year-old bridegroom. I asked what he
meant. He quoted the words said when the rings
are exchanged – 'All that I am I give to you' –
and added: 'But I don't know all that I am yet.
And when I find out, I have to marry that bit as
well.' What an insight – it applies whether you
are seventeen or forty-seven. As we go on
sharing ourselves more and more fully, we
never stop 'getting married'.*

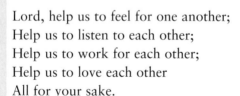

Lord, help us to feel for one another;
Help us to listen to each other;
Help us to work for each other;
Help us to love each other
All for your sake.

Women at Prayer

We've bought a house – what a big decision!
Can we afford it?
Have we chosen the right kind of mortgage?
Is it in the right place?
What will the neighbours be like?
This will be the house
    which will take most of our money
    where we will spend most of our time
      together
    where we will discover what living
      together is about
    where we may have our children.
Show us how to make our house
    into our home.

Andrew Body

✳

Blessing a home

At the threshold,
Through the hallway,
In the kitchen,
Come beside us.

In the place where we eat,
Be the silent guest at our meal.
In the space where we sit,
Be the friend who rests with us.
Where we wash, where we sleep,
May we know your care for us.

God of Peace, bless our house
And fill it with joy,
That here may visitors find a welcome
And generous refreshment.

Timothy Woods

Be with us as we make friends together. All our friends so far have known us as single people who have now got married. They are part of our past, and we bring them with us into our future. But now help us to add to them new friends who have only known us as a couple, and who see us, as we see ourselves, as one.

Andrew Body

＊

In a world where sex sells, is sold and
    becomes sordid,
where bare bodies create income,
    not intimacy,
thank you that in the closeness and
    commitment of our relationship
we have a glimpse of Eden,
where nakedness is natural
and love-making is a sacrament of love
    and unity.

Andrew Body

O Jesus, be the canoe that holds me up in
the sea of life;
Be the rudder that helps me in the
straight road;
Be the outrigger that supports me in times
of temptation;
Let your Spirit be my sail that carries me
through each day.
Keep my body strong, so I can paddle
steadfastly on in the voyage of life.

Melanesian prayer: from Women at Prayer

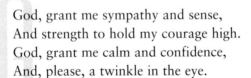

God, grant me sympathy and sense,
And strength to hold my courage high.
God, grant me calm and confidence,
And, please, a twinkle in the eye.

Women at Prayer

In the warmth of intimacy
And the fire of passion
We find our need of one another.
And we thank you, God, for the thrill of
    our union.
May the love that burns between us
Become a source of energy for those
    around us,
And the firmness of our commitment
Be a rock of support for our loved ones.
Use us, we pray,
To bring light to the world's greyness,
And warmth to the world's coolness.
In the name of Christ, who calls all people
    to life in its fullness.

Timothy Woods

Our loving Master and God, we thank you for making women and for the joy of being a wife and/or a mother. In these times, Lord, many women have to hold jobs or run businesses in addition to the arduous responsibilities of running their homes. We need your special grace and blessing to be able to be successful both at home and at work; we often neglect one for the other. Lord, help us so to organize and manage our time and homes that we will be able to progress at our various jobs. Give us the spirit and heart that is easily content with what has been given to us by you, so that we are not blinded by envy and selfish drives. We pray in Jesus' name.

Nigerian prayer: from Women at Prayer

So many times I've exploded inside –
'I'm just a doormat; people use me!'
And yet, Lord, a doormat has a place in
    your house.
It's a tough thing, a doormat: it takes a lot
    of battering,
but year after year it helps people remove
    the dirt and grime.
It stands at the entrance of the house:
people say, 'I won't come in, my shoes
    are dirty,'
and I say, 'Use the mat,' and in they come.
Sometimes people turn up and use its
    strong edge to pull off muddy boots,
and come inside with stockinged feet.
It sees the worst side of life, does a doormat.

Lord, help me to be a doormat.
Let me be strong and reassuring, to listen to
    people's troubles and worries;
to help them unload the things that keep
    them from your house.
For, Lord, I know I will not be weighed down
    for long; like a diligent housewife,
you will lift me up and beat me clean, and
    prepare me for the next time.

Lord, keep me constantly aware of that
    need for your care.
Without the constant beating and cleaning,
    a doormat soon becomes clogged
and starts giving out more dirt than it removes.

Lord, make me a clean and willing doormat;
but don't let me expect to be used
    continually.
My children, Lord, don't need a doormat:
    our house is their home.
In they come – muddy boots, dirty shoes,
    the lot.
They leap over the mat in their anxiety to
    be home.
It's frustrating, Lord – I shout out, 'Use the
    mat!' But it's too late.
Life's like that, Lord.
Some of us find it easy to enter your house,
and know that your love is for us all,
    however unclean;
but others, Lord, need a doormat at
    the entrance.
Lord, make me a doormat.

Pippa Body

Lord,
Are you receiving me?
I'm having a whale of a time,
It's tremendous!

Ken Walsh

May springs of life and love be ours,
Gushing forth with hope and gladness;
May streams of sparkling goodness flow
Into the lives of those around us.
Make us, good Lord, a deep well of peace,
And a torrent of joy for those around us.
Guide us, we pray, in Jesus' name.

Timothy Woods

Why is time in such short supply?
There seems to be a breakdown in the
    production line.
Try as we may, we can find only twenty-
    four hours a day.
We need time for work – more and more of
    it, it seems –
    time for hobbies
    time for exercise
    time for shopping
    time for housework
    time for gardening
    time for DIY
    time for friends
    time for family
    time for the children
    time for making love
    time for just chilling out
    time for sleep
    time for holidays
    time for each other
    time for God.
Lord, if you really can't provide us with
    more than twenty-four hours a day, at
    least help us to sort out how best to use
    what you *have* given us.

Andrew Body

God of compassion, whose Son Jesus
    Christ, the child of Mary,
shared the life of a home in Nazareth,
and on the cross drew the whole human
    family to himself:
strengthen us in our daily living
that in joy and in sorrow
we may know the power of your presence
to bind together and to heal;
through Jesus Christ your Son our Lord,
who is alive and reigns with you,
in the unity of the Holy Spirit,
one God, now and for ever.

Common Worship

✳

Lord, you have taught us
that all our doings without love are
    nothing worth:
send your Holy Spirit
and pour into our hearts that most
    excellent gift of love,
the true bond of peace and of all virtues,
without which whoever lives is counted
    dead before you.
Grant this for your only Son
    Jesus Christ's sake,
who is alive and reigns with you,
in the unity of the Holy Spirit,
one God, now and for ever.

Common Worship

God of our pilgrimage,
you have led us to the living water:
refresh and sustain us
as we go forward on our journey,
in the name of Jesus Christ our Lord.

Common Worship

TIMES OF CHANGE

All marriages have to change – and people find change either a threat or an opportunity. Some changes are forced on us by outside circumstances, some because of the way we develop as individuals. A proud new father told me that he had always thought his wife was wonderful, but in watching her care for their baby he had seen another whole dimension of how wonderful she was. Another told me how watching his wife cope with a child with a disability had deepened his love. All changes – good and bad – have the potential to enrich our relationships.

It's different
   now that you have got a new job
   now that we have no parents to visit
   now that you have passed your driving test
   now that you are ill
   now that you have taken up your
      new hobby
   now that you have found faith
   now that . . .

Once we had found the balance on the see-
    saw of our relationship,
we could take pleasure in the give and take.
We can't go back to that – change is a
    reality we have to live with.
Help us to find how to balance things again
    in a new way.

Andrew Body

Oh God, thank you for the child I carry.
I am in love with it as I am in love with my
husband and my life – and you.
I walk the world in wonder. I see it through
new eyes.
All is changed, subtly but stingingly
different. The beauty of sunlight upon the
grass, the feel of its warmth along my arms.
It is cradling me in tenderness as I shall
cradle this child one day.
I am mother and child in one, new as a child
myself, innocent, excited, amused, surprised.
I marvel at my changing body. It is as sweet
and new to me as when I was a little girl.

'See how important I am', my body claims.
'Feel my insistence as I make and shape this
child for you.'
Oh God, bless this body in which the
mystery of life is working. Let it be equal
to its job. And bless the tiny marvel it is
responsible for. Your handiwork! O bless
my baby too – let it be whole and beautiful
and strong.

Marjorie Holmes

God our Father,
maker of all that is living,
we praise you for the wonder and joy
    of creation.
We thank you from our hearts for the life
    of this child,
for a safe delivery and for the privilege
    of parenthood.
Accept our thanks and praise,
through Jesus Christ our Lord.

The Alternative Service Book

O Lord almighty, who hast made us out of nothing and redeemed us by the precious blood of thine only Son, preserve, I beseech thee, the work of thy hands and defend both me and the tender fruit of my womb from all perils and evils. I beg thee, for myself, thy grace, protection and a happy delivery; and for my child, that thou wouldest preserve it for baptism, sanctify it for thyself and make it thine for ever.

The Christian's Guide to Heaven (1794)

✻

Father God, give me a patient heart
When my love busies herself with
    household concerns;
A listening ear when she speaks of hope
    or disappointment;
A thick skin when she blames me for her woes.

Make me close enough to be ready to listen
    or laugh, watch or weep;
Make me detached enough to hear her
    beyond the words she speaks;
Help us to grow in love
That we may bring glory to your name.

Timothy Woods

God our Father
in giving us this child you have shown us
    your love.
Help us to be trustworthy parents.
Make us patient and understanding, that our
    child may always be sure of our love
and grow up to be happy and responsible,
through Jesus Christ our Lord.

*Thanksgiving after adoption:
from The Alternative Service Book*

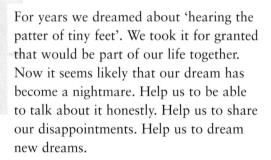

For years we dreamed about 'hearing the
patter of tiny feet'. We took it for granted
that would be part of our life together.
Now it seems likely that our dream has
become a nightmare. Help us to be able
to talk about it honestly. Help us to share
our disappointments. Help us to dream
new dreams.

Andrew Body

When the next generation moves away

Loving Father
I have always feared this day
and pretended, to myself,
       it would never come.

It is hard to watch one I love and treasure
set out to make an independent way in life.

Lord, I do not easily release my child into
       a harsh world,
yet I know *she/he* cannot stay under my
       wing for ever.

Growth and maturity demands
a leaving of the nest and a moving on.

Overshadow us with your protecting love
and give to each of us a loving heart,
a courageous spirit
and a life filled with your peace.
May our love for you and for each other
flourish and prosper.
Lord, hear my prayer.

Vows and Partings

An empty place at the table,
Silence from the bedroom – no loud music!
Clothes no longer strewn on the floor,
The washing machine strangely silent.
My child has gone away.

*'It was I who taught Ephraim to walk,
I took them up in my arms.'* Hosea 11.3

Loving God, you are Father and Mother to
        your children
And you have let them go –
To grow, to live, to learn.
Your children have always made mistakes,
Hurt themselves and others
And still you love them.

'How can I give you up, Ephraim?'
                    Hosea 11.8

Loving God,
Help me to let go,
To see that the house is empty
Because it is the launching pad to new life.

Loving God,
Help me to accept a relationship
        which is changing,
Allowing me space
And challenging me to embrace all the
        possibility of a new beginning.

Vows and Partings

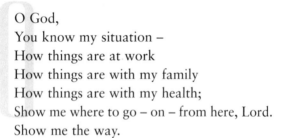

O God,
You know my situation –
How things are at work
How things are with my family
How things are with my health;
Show me where to go – on – from here, Lord.
Show me the way.

I don't ask to see the end of the road
Or even all the road.

Just enough, so that I'll know
In which direction
To move, now.

Ken Walsh

Leaving a home

Lord, this has been quite a house
in which to grow up
as parents and as children.

It has seen much laughter,
it has watched the shedding of many tears
and it has heard many an argument,
but now it is time to leave.

Help us to look back with gratitude –
to be gentle in our remembrances
and reserved in our judgements.
Let us be slow to condemn those who have
        lived here
and lenient on its occupants
where at first we might have apportioned
        blame.

Thank you for the warmth of this house,
for its character,
its friendliness and, above all,
for its patience with those who once
        lived here.

Vows and Partings

Gracious God, look on us in your love and give us your blessing. Be with N as *he/she* leaves us, and be with those of us who remain here. You know our feelings at this time. Help us to remember that we are always united to one another in your love, made known to us in Jesus Christ our Lord.

The Book of Alternative Services of
the Anglican Church of Canada 1985

✳

I'm starting work again tomorrow after ...
    years.
I'm excited, God, but oh, so scared!
I feel I'm out of date, but they did seem
    pleased to see me.
May I find fulfilment in this venturing out.
Lord God, help me to keep
    a right balance between
Family, home and work;
    help me to keep my priorities
Right so that home will continue to be a
    place of love and security.

Women at Prayer

Lord, as we go forward to retirement we
thank you for the blessing of past years.
Help us to adjust to our different lifestyle;
to grasp the new opportunities given,
remembering the needs of others; to use our
leisure creatively; and in the new-found joy
of time together, may we continue in your
love and service.

Women at Prayer

Loving Creator, it seems as though you've
given us a second chance. After all these
years of busy-ness, of deadlines, of demands,
of other's concerns; now, in our retirement,
at last we have time with each other. We can
enjoy the privilege of planning each day –
guide us as we plan. We can relax and take
outings – restore us in these times. We can
take up new hobbies and new interests – be
near us as we choose. May our retirement
be a time of re-creation, and in all we do
may we know your presence with us, your
love surrounding us to eternity.

Women at Prayer

Let nothing disturb you, nothing
    destroy you;
All things pass, but God never changes.
Whoever has God lacks nothing;
If you have only God, you have
    more than enough.

St Teresa of Avila

TIMES OF CONFLICT

Every marriage has its ups and downs.
The wedding service has its feet firmly on the
ground, with its talk of 'for better for worse,
for richer for poorer, in sickness and in health'.
A couple once wanted to include W. H. Auden' s
poem 'Tell me the truth about love' in their
wedding, but wanted to change the line 'when
it comes, will it come without warning, just as
I'm picking my nose?' to 'just as I'm picking a
rose?' That is a romantic and unrealistic view
of marriage. The service is down to earth, and
'picking my nose' is nearer the mark, as well
as being what the poet wrote!

*

God of love, she does not share my love for
   you, she does not know
   the freedom that comes from trusting you:
   the freedom from fear,
   the freedom to abandon all cares and
      anxieties into your hands;
she does not know
   the peace and serenity of your presence,
   the assurance of your divine love;
she tolerates my religious activities.

Lord, whether or not she accepts you is
      between you and her.
Grant that my love for you will not be a
      threat to her.
Grant me the wisdom to love and love so
      that she will
want to share my knowledge and faith in you.
One day, dear God, may we walk
      with you together.

Women at Prayer

Many years ago I decided that when I was married I was definitely not going to be a nagging wife. The other day I listened to myself talking to my husband and I realized with horror that was just what I was doing ... nagging, niggling, needling. I decided to see if the Bible has anything to say on this subject – yes, it never fails. There were quite a few comments in Proverbs. Here are some from *The Living Bible*:

'It is better to live in the corner of an attic than with a crabby woman in a lovely home.' (21.9)

'... and nagging wife annoys like constant dripping.' (19.13)

'A constant dripping on a rainy day and a cranky woman are much alike' (27.15)

The message is clear, Lord.
Stop nagging or be a drip.

Help me.

Women at Prayer

Lord I am angry with . . .
not just irritated
but deep down angry.
Thank you for this anger, without it
I would be anaemic.
Thank you for showing me how I feel,
for otherwise it would be focused on those
who are not the objects of it.
But now, now what shall I do with it,
        Lord?
Anger let out can be so destructive,
things can be said which are
        never forgotten.
But it can't stay bottled up in me.
I commit my anger into your hands, Lord.
Take my anger, transmute it into something
no less vital, but stronger and deeper.

Richard Harries

I will trust in the Lord to bring joy back
into my marriage.
I am so lonely. My husband is so lonely.
We can't talk to each other any more.
There is so little touching between us.
We can't reach out any more.
We pass like ships on a dark night at sea,
fearful of drawing too close lest we crash.
There is a great fog between us. We call
out to each other, but the fog of our
different interests and many concerns
blurs the message.
The sound is harsh and forlorn.
It is meaningless.
Even the occasions when we try to come
together as man and wife are meaningless.
It is worse than if we were strangers:
strangers would take some interest in each
other. But although we are supposed to
love each other, and do, there is no interest,
no delight.
Lord, let the light of your presence bring
joy back into our marriage. Burn bright
within each of us, to warm us and cheer us
so that it breaks down the fog between us.
Dear Lord, shine through me as a person to
reach my husband and draw close to him in
love and joy, the way you meant us to.

Marjorie Holmes

Bless every circumstance of this, my life.
Bless the bad of it as well as the good of it.
For out of the bad of it will surely come
further good.
Out of its problems I will arise stronger.
Out of its sorrows I will emerge wiser and
purer and better equipped to cope with
what is yet to come.
Even my family will benefit from these
troubles and trials, for in them they too
are being tested.
They will emerge better, stronger people.
They will become more mature. For their
life stories are being written in blood and
fire as well as love.
God, help us all to see these truths.
Bless us in our hours of family affliction.
Though they may be hours that separate us
now, bless them ... bless them.

Marjorie Holmes

How can I picture our relationship, Lord?
At this moment, it feels like a cracked tea-cup.
But what kind of cup is it?
Is it one from the supermarket, or from
      Meissen or Wedgwood?
If it were cheap, we would throw it away;
but if it were valuable, we would
      get it repaired.
What we have had is precious, Lord,
so help us to make the repairs,
to acknowledge our part in the damage,
and to work at making it right again.

Andrew Body

*

Lord Christ, enable us to place our trust
      in you,
and so to live in the present moment.
So often we forget that you never want human
suffering, but peace in our hearts.
Christ Jesus, by your Spirit you dwell in us.
More still, you pray in us.
Your miracle within us is accomplished
through the trust we have in you
and your continual forgiveness.

Brother Roger: from Praying Together in Word and Song

Jesus, Risen Lord,
you change and transfigure our heart just
    as it is.
You do not even ask us to uproot
    the weeds;
you take care of that.
With our own wounds, the thorns that
    hurt us, you
light a fire – and a way forward opens
    in us to
welcome your Spirit of compassion and
    the Spirit of
praise that brings healing.
So that what is most resistant in us,
    our failures,
our refusals and our inner abysses,
    may be transfigured
into energies of love and reconciliation;
all that you ask of us is that
    we welcome you
and rejoice in the miracle
    of your forgiveness.

Brother Roger; from Praying Together in Word and Song

God of peace
We have a deep desire to live in harmony
    with those close to us,
Yet conflicts arise from expectations,
    demands, hopes and fears.
Unite us in facing the causes of these
    present difficulties,
Help us to acknowledge the hurt we have
    inflicted on each other,
And the pain we have had to endure;
Enable us to let go of the wrongs so that
    no bitterness remains
And give us grace to forgive and to receive
    forgiveness.

Vows and Partings

Lord, when I feel myself sliding into the pit
... stay close; sit with me in my silence and
confusion, and give me your shoulder to
lean on. Prevent me from falling too far,
and, in your good time, help me to rise to
my feet again, in Jesus' name.

Women at Prayer

Teach us, Jesus, to let go
Of the small things that irritate us in our
    loved one's eyes.
And help us to do something about the
    planks in our own.
Give us, Teacher, the spirit of generosity
That will not judge the other harshly,
For we ourselves will be judged in turn.
So lead us in the paths of humility,
Ready always to give of ourselves to the other,
to enrich and to strengthen them,
that our lives may be songs of praise to you
Today and for ever.

Timothy Woods

✳

O God,
you know us to be set
in the midst of so many and great dangers,
that by reason of the frailty of our nature
we cannot always stand upright:
grant to us such strength and protection
as may support us in all dangers
and carry us through all temptations;
through Jesus Christ your Son our Lord,
who is alive and reigns with you,
in the unity of the Holy Spirit,
one God, now and for ever.

Common Worship

Almighty God,
you see that we have no power of ourselves
    to help ourselves:
keep us both outwardly in our bodies,
and inwardly in our souls;
that we may be defended from all adversities
which may happen to the body,
and from all evil thoughts which may
    assault and hurt the soul;
through Jesus Christ our Lord.

Common Worship

O God,
this journey we started out on,
well, it's got a lot harder lately.

It seemed so easy when we set off,
but lately the going's got tougher,
and it's a struggle.

I knew it would sometimes be uphill
but I didn't think it would be so hard:
sometimes I feel almost alone
    taken for granted,
        taken for a ride, even.

But listen, God,
I'm pressing on
because at the top of this next hill
there's a great view
where we can sit down together
and look back encouraged
to see how far we've already come
and get a glimpse
    of the wonderful path ahead:
it shouldn't be surprising
    that the steepest hills
and the toughest paths
give the most rewarding views.

O God keep our gaze high
    our hearts brave
        and our legs strong.

Peter Coley

SPECIAL TIMES

I would be hard pressed to find something that gives me more 'job satisfaction' than officiating at weddings – but maybe it is topped by celebrations of anniversaries, when so often couples speak so movingly of their ups and downs, and how they have found God's presence with them through the years. Few brides are able to wear their wedding dress on their golden anniversary, but I did have a groom who put on the very same pair of shoes he had worn fifty years before. Whatever our special times, it is good to find a way of offering them to God, in public or in private. Common Worship provides an outline to help plan a public celebration; maybe these prayers can help you to find words to use in private.

✳

Reaffirmation of vows

Gracious God
we thank you for your presence
    in our marriage
and for the love, joy and friendship we
    have known.
We praise you for your guidance
    in times of discovery and change,
for your comfort in times of sadness,
and for your strength in times of weakness.

Vows and Partings

*

Any wedding anniversary

Gracious God, on this special day we
remember with thanksgiving our vows of
love and commitment to you and to each
other in marriage. We pray for your
continued blessing. May we learn from both
our joys and our sorrows, and discover new
riches in our life together in you. We ask
this in the name of Jesus Christ our Lord.

*The Book of Alternative Services of the Anglican
Church of Canada 1985*

SOME ANNIVERSARY PRAYERS

First anniversary – Cotton

After a year, we're just beginning to cotton
on to what marriage is about. Thank you
for all the new things we are discovering
about each other, when we thought we
knew each other so well. Bind us closer
and closer, like the cotton which keeps
the buttons on our clothes.

Second anniversary – Paper

It's there for all to see on the certificate –
we are husband and wife. But those are
only marks on a paper. Help us, today and
every day, to make our marriage real – or
it won't be worth the paper it is written on.

Third anniversary – Leather

The bikers are safer inside their armour
of leather – protected from the grazes and
knocks that are bound to happen. Make
our relationship as tough as that – no,
better – make it as tough as old boots,
to cope with whatever life throws at us.

Fourth anniversary – Books

Thank you that we are sharing the books of our lives. Thank you for what we have learned from each other. Thank you for the poetry of our love. Thank you for the history with which we enrich each other. Thank you that the story has only just begun, and we cannot guess how it will turn out.

Fifth anniversary – Wood

The tree grows a new ring each year. How big it is depends on the weather. Thank you for the things that have helped us grow during these last five years. May our sapling marriage grow into a mighty trunk that has firm roots in your love.

Sixth anniversary – Iron

Our relationship is so strong. Help us to cherish it, so that it never goes rusty. Thank you that we can be for each other that other kind of iron – getting rid of the creases that make things less than perfect.

Seventh anniversary – Wool

There is something very cosy about being close together – and we really do know that 'we've got our love to keep us warm'. But help us never to try to pull the wool over each other's eyes.

Eighth anniversary – Bronze

Copper and tin are both useful metals. But together they make one which is beautiful and rich. Thank you that because we are together, we become something greater than we could ever be on our own.

Ninth anniversary – Copper

Copper wires are great at conducting electricity. Help us to empower each other in our daily lives. Copper is soft, and easily shaped: help us to learn to compromise and be what each other needs. And as the years go by, help us to acquire that rich patina which makes things even more wonderful.

Tenth anniversary – Tin

They've found tins on the mountains left by expeditions years and years ago – and the food inside them is still fresh and nutritious. As we reach our 'double figures', help us to keep our relationship fresh and good.

Fifteenth anniversary – Crystal

Thank you for all that is crystal clear in our life, for the assurance we have of each other's love. As we gaze into the crystal ball of the future, which only you know, help us to trust that you will go on being with us as you have been in the past.

Twentieth anniversary – China

The finest china ultimately comes from the clay of the earth. Thank you that out of the ordinary people we are, you have helped us to make something beautiful.

Twenty-fifth anniversary — Silver

The alchemists said that silver represented the moon, and that has always been a romantic image, from honeymoons onward. Keep us full of romance and passion and wonder, however old we live to be.

Thirtieth anniversary — Pearl

Sometimes grit can stop a machine. Sometimes, in an oyster, it enables a beautiful pearl to form. Help us to make the best we can of what life throws at us.

Thirty-fifth anniversary — Coral

Coral is a living thing which grows in beauty as the years go by. May that be the story of our relationship.

Fortieth anniversary — Ruby

The ancients thought that ruby was the antidote to poisons, and could banish grief. May our love continue to deal with all the imperfections that could spoil our happiness.

Forty-fifth anniversary – Sapphire

You can see through the most beautiful
sapphires – and yet they have a colour
that is unique. Help us to see the world
through each other's eyes, and to find
new glories in it every day.

Fiftieth anniversary – Gold

Just as silver represented the moon to the
alchemists, so gold represented the sun.
Thank you that we have been able to
bring light and warmth to each other
through the years. Thank you that our
love is so precious.

Andrew Body

PARTINGS

The wedding service says 'till death us do part'.
All marriages have to end one day, and sadly
some die before there is a physical death. Being
able to be thankful for what has been good is
a great gift at such times. To my amazement,
a man who had nursed his wife through fifteen
years of debilitating illness, which had begun
soon after their marriage, said 'I couldn't have
had a happier marriage.' That was taking 'for
better for worse, for richer for poorer, in
sickness and in health' really seriously.

*

I lived on my own for years.
I'm used to being content with
        my own company.
But it's all different now.
With these business trips, I don't feel alone –
I feel lonely.
I sometimes even feel resentful.
Help me to turn those feelings
into gratitude for what being together means.
Help me to move from loneliness
to joyful reunion.

Andrew Body

I let go
window and door
house and home
memory and fear.
I let go the hurt of the past
and look to the hope of the future.
I let go
knowing that I will always carry
part of my past (part of you) with me
woven into the story of my life.

Help me, Christ my brother
to softly fold inside
the grief and the sadness;
to pack away the pain
and to move on;
taking each day in your company
travelling each step
in your love.

The Iona Community: from The Pattern of our Days

Merciful God
For the things we have done that we regret,
forgive us;
for the things we have failed to do
    that we regret,
forgive us;
for all the times we have acted without love,
forgive us;
for all the times we have reacted
    without thought,
forgive us;
for all the times we have withdrawn care,
forgive us;
for all the times we have failed to forgive,
forgive us;

For hurtful words said
    and helpful words unsaid
for unfinished tasks
and unfulfilled hopes,
God of all time
forgive us,
and help us
to lay down our burden of regret.

The Iona Community: from The Pattern of our Days

Loving God,
we feel hollow and empty,
with intentions and expectations, hopes and
    dreams unfulfilled;
we had expected our love for each other to
    last for ever;
that it would draw us ever closer,
and sustain us through bad times
    as well as good.
Once it flourished, but now it has withered
    and died
like a flower of the field, it is gone.

Forgive us that we no longer look to you
to bless and renew us in our partnership.
In your mercy, hear us,
as we pray for healing and renewal
    in our separation.

In the days to come
raise us up to new life
in fresh relationships.

Make us gentler in our ways
and altogether more understanding.

Vows and Partings

God of mercy and compassion
forgive me the hurt I have caused to those
    I have loved.
Forgive the angry words,
    the bitter thoughts,
the resentment that wells up within me.
Forgive me when others have been caught
    up in our arguments:
friends, parents, children.
Help me to learn how to forgive as I live
    with my regrets.
Help me to restore relationships
with those whose trust in me
    has been damaged.

Vows and Partings

Gracious God
we remember our years together,
in which we have grown and changed.
We pray for each other as we separate.
May we be enriched by our happy memories
and let go of our painful ones.
Bless us both in our life journeys,
and give us confidence to walk into the future
strengthened by the time we have shared,
and with each other's blessing.

Vows and Partings

Loving God
as I grieve for the relationship
    that has now ended
help me to give thanks for all that was good
without clinging to the past;
help me to put aside all that was hurtful
not allowing bitterness to cloud the present;
above all, help me to look to the future
    with hope
and believe in the possibility
    of a new beginning.

Vows and Partings

FURTHER MARRIAGE

*Sharing the heartache of bereavement or divorce
takes you to some of the most profound agonies
people have to go through. But then to see
people find love again can be like watching
the sun transforming a grey day. God is there
– however it looks – but to hear someone say
'God has led me to ... and has helped me
through great pain, and to come to terms with
what has happened in the past' is to have the
privilege of watching God's healing at work.*

Loving God,
you are merciful and forgiving.
Grant that those who are suffering the
     hurts of the past may experience your
     generous love.
Heal their memories, comfort them,
and send them all from here
renewed and hopeful;
in Jesus Christ our Lord.

A Prayer Book for Australia

God of all grace and goodness,
we thank you for this new family,
and for everything parents and children
    have to share;
by your Spirit of peace draw them together
and help them to be true friends
    to one another.
Let your love surround them
and your care protect them,
through Jesus Christ our Lord.

A Prayer Book for Australia

*

Lord,
this is a new family.
We have different stories that have brought
    us to this place,
but now we are bound together.

Give us
    patience when one of us gets things wrong;
    tolerance when one of us talks about the
      way things were;
    and understanding, when we disagree
      because we always used to do things
      differently.

Help us to care for each other,
enjoy each other
and learn to love each other.

Vows and Partings

In the stillness of this moment I hold my
breath, and marvel at the wonder of this
second chance in marriage.

God thank you for this second time of
marriage. We each accept all that has gone
before. We pledge ourselves to this new
love. May our experiences and differences
take on a positive value, that through them
we may enrich our lives as we learn from
one another.

Thank you for our past, for the pains and
for the joys.

Thank you for your blessing on us now.
May we continue to know this blessing and
may it always be part of our lives together.

Women at Prayer

Prayers for every day

Whatever stage of our marriage we may be at, we have the opportunity to bring each other and our relationship to God each day. We can bring our past, our present and our future to him, knowing that his love is unchanging and unchangeable – as the writer of 'Lamentations' in the Old Testament said, it is 'new every morning'. Prayers at special times are important, but sharing every day with God is best of all. All of us could improve on the grace one of our children brought back from playgroup: 'Hands together, eyes closed, stick your fingers up your nose'!

The night has passed, and the day lies open
before us;
let us pray with one heart and mind.
[*Silence is kept.*]
As we rejoice in the gift of this new day,
so may the light of your presence, O God,
set our hearts on fire with love for you;
now and for ever.

Common Worship: Daily Prayer

O Lord our God, who hast chased the slumber from our eyes, accept our prayers and supplications, and give us faith that maketh not ashamed, confident hope and love unfeigned; bless our coming in and going out, our thoughts, words and works, and grant us to begin, continue and end this day with the praise of the unspeakable sweetness of thy mercy.

Greek Liturgy

✳

O Lord, thou knowest how busy I must be this day. If I forget thee, do not thou forget me.

Sir Jacob Astley
(On the eve of the battle of Edgehill, 23 October 1642)

✳

Keep me as the apple of an eye.
Hide me under the shadow of thy wings.

The medieval late evening service of Compline

Go before us, Lord, in all we do
with your most gracious favour,
and guide us with your continual help,
that in all our works
begun, continued and ended in you,
we may glorify your holy name,
and finally by your mercy receive
    everlasting life;
through Jesus Christ our Lord.

Common Worship

*

Lighten our darkness, we beseech thee,
    O Lord;
and by thy great mercy defend us
from all perils and dangers of this night;
for the love of thy only Son, our Saviour,
    Jesus Christ.

The Book of Common Prayer

*

Pardon the folly of this short prayer; even
for Jesus Christ's sake. And give us a good
night, if it be thy pleasure.

Oliver Cromwell

O Lord and heavenly Father, we thy
humble servants entirely desire thy fatherly
goodness mercifully to accept this our
sacrifice of praise and thanksgiving; most
humbly beseeching thee to grant, that by
the merits and death of thy Son Jesus
Christ, and through faith in his blood,
we and all thy whole Church may obtain
remission of our sins, and all other benefits
of his passion. And here we offer and
present unto thee, O Lord, ourselves, our
souls and bodies, to be a reasonable, holy,
and lively sacrifice unto thee; humbly
beseeching thee, that all we, who are
partakers of this holy Communion, may
be fulfilled with thy grace and heavenly
benediction. And although we be
unworthy, through our manifold sins, to
offer unto thee any sacrifice, yet we
beseech thee to accept this our bounden
duty and service; not weighing our merits,
but pardoning our offences, through Jesus
Christ our Lord; by whom, and with
whom, in the unity of the Holy Ghost,
all honour and glory be unto thee,
O Father Almighty, world without end.

General Thanksgiving, The Book of Common Prayer

In your mercy
forgive what we have been,
help us to amend what we are,
and direct what we shall be;
that we may do justly,
love mercy,
and walk humbly with you, our God.

Common Worship: Daily Prayer

O God our protector,
by whose mercy the world turns safely
    into darkness
and returns again to light:
we give into your hands
    our unfinished tasks,
our unsolved problems,
and our unfulfilled hopes:
for you alone are our sure defence
and bring us lasting peace
in Jesus Christ our Lord.

Common Worship: Daily Prayer

INDEX OF FIRST LINES

INDEX OF AUTHORS AND SOURCES

Authors and Sources

ACKNOWLEDGEMENTS

The compilers and publisher gratefully acknowledge permission to reproduce copyright material in this anthology. Every effort has been made to trace and contact copyright holders. If there are any inadvertent omissions we apologize to those concerned and will ensure that a suitable acknowledgement is made at the next reprint.

The Anglican Church in Aotearoa, New Zealand: from *A New Zealand Prayer Book – He Karikia Mihinare O Aotearoa*, copyright © The Church of the Province of New Zealand 1989 (p. 9).

The Anglican Church of Australia: from *A Prayer Book for Australia*, copyright © The Anglican Church of Australia Trust Corporation 1995 (pp. 73–4).

The Archbishops' Council of the Church of England: from *The Alternative Service Book of the Church of England 1980*, copyright © 1980 (p. 39); *Common Worship: Services and Prayers for the Church of England*, copyright © 2000 (pp. 33–4, 56, 57); *Common Worship: Pastoral Services*, copyright © 2000 (pp. 3, 7, 10) and *Common Worship: Daily Prayer* (preliminary edition), copyright © 2002 (pp. 76, 80).

The Canterbury Press: from *An Order of Marriage for Christians from Different Churches*, The Joint Liturgical Group of Great Britain, copyright © 1999 (p. 20).
Peter Coley (pp. 57–8).
Continuum Book Publishing Ltd: from *Praying Together in Word and Song*, Taizé, copyright © 1981 (pp. 53–4).
The General Synod of the Anglican Church of Canada: prayers adapted from *Occasional Celebrations*, copyright © 1992 (pp. 44, 60).
The Rt Revd Richard Harries (p. 50).
Hodder & Stoughton Ltd: from *I've Got to Talk to Somebody, Lord* by Marjorie Holmes, copyright © 1968 (pp. 36–7).
Trustees for Methodist Church Purposes: from *Vows and Partings*, copyright © 2001; used by permission of Methodist Publishing House (pp. 5, 40, 41–2, 43, 55, 60, 70, 71, 72, 74–5).
Ken Walsh (pp. 31, 42).
Wild Goose Publication: from the Iona Community from *The Pattern of our Days*, copyright © 1996 (pp. 17, 68, 69).
Timothy Woods (pp. 13, 24, 27, 31, 38, 56).
The Zondervan Corporation: from *Women at Prayer* by Rachel Stowe, copyright © 1994, used by permission (pp. 4, 22, 26, 28, 44, 45, 48, 49, 55, 75).